glitter books

DIANA
THE LAST 24 HOURS

Allan Silverman

ISBN 1-902588-00-2

Published by The Glitter Books of London.

DIANA
THE LAST 24 HOURS

ALLAN SILVERMAN

Paris, August 31, 1997.

The air is dusty with traffic haze. Most of the city's inhabitants are holidaying in the South. The sultry weather promises thunder, but not of the kind that is to come later that night with the impacted force of a Mercedes 280-S limo crashing at high speed into the thirteenth pillar of a Paris underpass.

Diana's notorious love-life has carried her through years of mismatched affairs to the arms of an infatuated Dodi Fayed. After the emotional bankruptcy of her ill-fated marriage to Charles, Diana is in pursuit of what she knows best: hedonistic pleasure. For once in her life, she has met an individual whose tastes for self-indulgence are as limitless as her own. Dodi lacks public profile. He is a dilettante, exceedingly wealthy, but without the talent necessary to bring him any form of artistic distinction. His attachment to Diana promises to elevate his frustratingly low status in society.

Dodi's plush Paris apartment, situated high above the Champs Elysées, and overlooking the Arc de Triomphe is the ideal love-nest for the couple to share for the evening of their final day. There have been reports that summer of Dodi having his chauffeurs drive the couple at life-endangering speed from one secret rendezvous to another. This game, rather like Russian roulette, has contributed to their mutual search for sensational thrills. It's in the air, that a fatal accident may occur.

Dodi's apartment is a fitting refuge for a Princess accustomed to a lifestyle of unbridled luxury. The bedroom wardrobes are stuffed with her pristine-condition designer gowns.

The apartment boasts a king-size bed with a silk canopy and ornate headboard. Diana has placed one of her teddy bears on top of a mound of fancy cushions. In the marbled bathroom the lovers have hung their two peach coloured towelling his-and-hers robes, side by side. The huge round bath has gold plated taps, and Diana's toiletries occupy every available shelf-space. Diana has placed a cuddly rabbit on the bathroom's velvet couch, as a symbol of the girliness to which Dodi is devoted. Diana has spent her public life being analysed, dissected, and photographed by the media. It's impossible to tell whether it is she or they who have instigated what has become over the years a 24-hour PR machine. At least here in Dodi's apartment, she is free from both attracting and demanding media attention. Diana suffers withdrawal symptoms if she's not continually in the public eye. She's a media-junkie, and Dodi is more than anxious to cultivate his own desires to become similarly addicted. Both of them are desirous, despite their protests to the contrary, to publicise their romance to a sensation-hungry press.

The apartment is screened from traffic noise, and Dodi, whose habit has him flying high, is busy enthusing over every aspect of their planned future together. It's early days, but the passion they have shared for the past month, together with the commingling of two vast fortunes, appears to invite prospects of illustrious bonding. Diana keeps a treasured silver plaque inscribed with a poem from Dodi under her pillow, and he gives pride of place to a cigar cutter with a gold tag inscribed "with love from Diana". The couple have characteristically expressed their love for each other through silver and gold, metals that may be seen as implying the marriage of the moon and sun. Diana is the lunar goddess, and Dodi the solar king. Together they see their wealth as rivalling the heavenly bodies.

Earlier in the evening there's been a tantrum

on Diana's part. She has discovered a wad of love letters sent to Dodi by one of his ongoing stable of lovers. The letters are too steamily explicit for Dodi to make light of them, and there's a brief fracas over whether or not he is capable of proving faithful, should the lovers go ahead with their plans to marry. Diana's experiences with Charles' undying passion for Camilla Parker Bowles, have taught her that men are never to be trusted. Dodi's track-record as an international playboy has given her adequate cause for suspicion. His abilities to perform are hot gossip in Parisian circles. Diana has succeeded in landing her man, but she is still unsure of his capacities for devotion. She wants to love him unconditionally, but she is frightened of going for that last fraction of marital commitment. There is a brief disagreement which is quickly resolved by physical passion. The letters turn out to have been written by Marie Bijou, the daughter of Antoine Bijou, wine-merchant, and one of Dodi's more recent conquests. Her nearby apartment, also in the Champs Elysées, seems too dangerously close for Diana's safety. Marie who was immediately to leave Paris after the fatal crash, is a Parisienne blonde, who in defiance of her Sorbonne education had spent her student years stripping in a sleazy club. Diana is to discover in the letters reference to Dodi's performance in bed, as well as playful allusions to Dodi's having asked for her hand in marriage. Marie had written of car rides across Paris with Dodi, and of the couple being out of their minds on recreational drugs.

This momentary intrusion of their shared bliss has been patched up in bed. Dodi's tender advances and sweet admissions of love would conquer any woman's heart, let alone a Princess starved of affection for years by an intolerable marriage. Dodi teaches her new techniques of love-making, introducing ideas that Charles would never have been adventurous enough to suggest. Diana is prepared to drop the issue of Marie Bijou, as they relax in a heavily scented bubble-bath. They are in heaven, as they sip champagne, and return again to the theme of marriage. Unknown to Diana, Dodi has already bought an engagement ring, and is preparing to pop the question later that night over dinner at the Ritz Hotel. His heart is in his mouth at the prospects of unifying the Al Fayeds and

Spencers in one of the biggest publicity scoops of the century. But it's also Diana's turn to reproach Dodi for the secret love affair he has been conducting with Kelly Fisher, an American model, parallel to their own scorching summer romance. She has every reason to feel aggrieved, for Dodi has on occasions established the two women in one residence, and treated the American as a plaything, while avowing romantic love to Diana. Diana is discovering for herself the complexities that come of mature relationships, when a complicated personal history makes it difficult for either partner to offer absolute commitment.

The atmosphere in the flat is still one of tension brewing for a storm. Kelly Fisher has been trying to get through to Dodi for days, and the telephone suddenly coming alive simultaneous with a stormy moment has Diana automatically jump to the conclusion that the caller can be no other than Kelly.

Diana shrieks, "I'll get it," and rushes to collect the call. "If it's that flaming bitch again," she adds, but the telephone goes dead before she can reach it. Dodi pours himself a large brandy, and tries to pretend that none of this is happening. He can sniff another scene in the making, and quickly shifts the subject to passions that they have in common, like shopping in the Faubourg Saint-Germain, oodles of travel talk, and starting a new family. Their whirlwind romance has permitted little serious discussion, and Diana is reminded of the equally surface relations that succeeded in killing her marriage to Charles. While Dodi compensates for shallow emotions with physical passion, Diana has known this sort of man before, and is wary of a quick-fling mentality. The two lovers find themselves embracing, but remain unable to penetrate a deeper level of communication. In the past months Diana's designers have grown scared of the quantity and quality of clothes she is beginning to require. Her rapacious spending-sprees are proving embarrassing even to her couturists, many of whom risk bankruptcy, should Diana prove fickle and cancel an extravagant order. Diana, like someone revealing a rare archive, now introduces Dodi to her latest shoe purchases from Malaysian born Jimmy Choo. She likes to tell Dodi of how she would have Choo drive to Kensington Palace, armed with samples of shapes, colours and fabrics, and of how together they would decide on creations for her perfect size six feet. To get rid of some of the tension in the air surrounding Diana's suspicions that Dodi has every intention of continuing his affair with Kelly Fisher, she loads Dodi's arms with her recent purchases. Dodi discovers that the satin, strappy sandals that Diana buys in such quantity carry the royal insignia on their inner soles. Diana is planning to have another two hundred pairs made for her in the coming months. Jimmy is her sort of chap, and she tells Dodi that he too must have his shoes designed by the Malaysian maestro. Diana disapproves of Dodi's preference for sportswear, and complains that he is dumbing down her image as an international fashion leader. She compares Dodi's lack of taste to the fashion-consciousness of her close friend Elton John, and suggests that Dodi should also wear pink, lilac and lime-green Versace suits. Elton, Diana continues, "is a real breezer, and has snorted more quantities of drugs in his life than Yardleys have manufactured talcum powder". She wants to play the album "Made In England", and finds it among a clutter of CDs with which she travels. Never far from her side are records by her favourite popular artists, Dire Straits, Simply Red, Eric Clapton, Phil Collins, George Michael, and Michael Jackson. Diana's tastes are for MOR artists. She also likes the Christian pop star, Adrian Snell, who once gave a private charity concert for her in a London Hotel. Diana was there when Snell performed at a concert in Peterborough Cathedral to save money for the Leprosy Mission, in 1991. She places Snell's CDs "Feed The Hungry Heart" and "Kiss The Tears" on the couch, next to a number of albums by Chris de Burgh and Elton John.

When Dodi asks her about Adrian Snell, she professes an admiration for the compassion he succeeds in conveying in songs like "Feed The Hungry Heart", and Dodi requests to hear the singer and song writer from Bath's opus after they have listened to Elton John's new offering. Diana warns Dodi that Snell's music makes her cry, and that perhaps they should listen on another occasion. "We are not playing Adrian and disagreeing," she says, and curls up on the sofa to enjoy Elton's rumbustious ballads.

The couple are almost immediately

interrupted in their listening by a call from Diana's intimate confidante, Lady Bowker. Diana is quick to respond. "Elsa, I adore him. I've never been so happy," the Princess says to Lady Bowker. She goes on to joke with Bowker, that the initials on her gilt belt read CC. "No, darling, it is not Coco Channel," she laughs, "it is Camilla and Charles."

Dodi starts to glow at the realisation that the Princess's love for him is helping her reconcile her differences with Camilla Parker Bowles, Tiggy Legge-Bourke and the Prince of Wales.

Diana tells Lady Bowker that she can't wait to see her again in the latter's London apartment in Eton Square, as she may have some very important news to convey. The Princess is glad that she has avoided being in Britain in July, for the Prince has hosted a 50th birthday party for Parker Bowles at Highgrove, his country home. "Wouldn't it be funny if I suddenly came out of the birthday cake," Diana jokes with Elsa. The conversation switches to Diana's resentment about Tiggy Leggy-B's intimate friendship with William, 15, and Harry, 12. Diana is furious that Legge-Bourke has referred to the two boys as "my babies", but is now prepared to forgive this mark of indiscretion on Tiggy's part. Diana reconsiders the matter and imparts to Lady Bowker her feelings that Tiggy "is devoted to the children and they are devoted to her. Because she gives them happiness, I now accept her."

Dodi pours himself another brandy, and hears his lover confide her real feelings of insecurity. Diana holds his hand, as she tells Elsa Bowker, "I've always been unwanted. I was unwanted as a baby because my parents wanted a boy, and I've been unwanted in my marriage because Charles loved someone else. I've been starved of love and affection, Elsa, but now I've got this real hon and he is sitting beside me."

Bowker consoles Diana in her accustomed, maternal way, and hears the Princess pour her heart out over the problems of lack of privacy in her life. In an effort to escape the unrelenting media attention and daily intrusions in her life, Diana threatens to consider moving from Britain to live in South Africa. "You know how I hate formality," Diana confides. "All I want is some privacy with darling Dodi. And perhaps two daughters, Elsa. A new start. But I wouldn't really leave Britain."

When Diana puts the phone down, Dodi is able to see that she is relieved for having spoken of her intimate concerns over family. Diana needs to periodically offload her anxieties, otherwise she develops eating disorders, and her much publicised problems with bulimia have had the media keep a constant eye on her figure and weight. In recent weeks, holidaying on the Emerald Coast, the half-mile long beach in the Cala di Volpe of Sardinia, Diana has regularly been photographed wearing white or beige shorts, with skimpy black or white summer tops. Her face has appeared drained of the anxieties that marked it during her unhappy marriage to Charles. There is every suggestion that love and the exhilarating coast have restored the Princess's radiance, and that her looks have returned to resembling the English rose that she so typifies.

We will leave the lovers in Dodi's luxurious Champs Elysées apartment, and familiarise ourselves with events leading up to the couple's arrival in Paris.

On Friday, August 29th, Dodi's 60-meter yacht the Jonikal has anchored at the Cala di Volpe, after a week's cruising the Emerald Coast. From the Cote d'Azur to the Costa photographers have pursued the couple in speed boats, on motor bikes, in cars, whatever it takes. Their singular aim is to find some flaw in the courting couple, and to media-expose it to the world.

Unnoticed by Diana and Dodi, two Italian photographers, Salvo la Fata and

Riccardo Frezza, have managed to steal up on the yacht in a small boat. They have been waiting around the yacht for days, observing Diana's every movement, and hoping that the couple would eventually come on land, or that they would get a shot of Diana topless. Now they have the chance – Diana dives into the water right in front of their lenses. They begin shooting, and immediately other paparazzi waiting on the shore, put out in small boats and jostle for positions. Luigi del Telvere, the Jonikal's Italian skipper, shouts at the intruders to go away and Diana disappears from on deck. The couple vanishing below deck is also a saucy reminder to the press that they are on the high seas for romance and love.

On the Friday morning Gian Franco Pes, 42, the official in charge of private flights at Olbia's airport receives a call informing him that a group of elite VIPs are to leave the airport the next day. He is told that there is to be no usual passport controls and that the party are to be driven direct to the aircraft. Flight details are confirmed and the plane, a Gulfstream-IV registration G-HARF is scheduled to take off the next day at 1.04 p.m. local time. Pez is informed that the mystery passenger is to be no other than Princess Diana, and that the accompanying bodyguard on board the flight is to be Trevor Rees-Jones.

After a steamy night of passion and hours of whispering sweet nothings to each other, the couple enjoy a late breakfast, and at noon the next day dock their launch at the jetty poking out from the Cala di Volpe hotel.

After a tense, but intimate series of confidences, Diana, dressed in a loose-fitting beige trouser suit designed by Catherine Walker, hurries out of the hotel lobby accompanied by Dodi. They jump into Tomas Muzzi's white Mercedes VIP taxi accompanied by Trevor Rees-Jones, Dodi's personal bodyguard and make a dash along the coast from Cala di Volpe to Olbia airport. Rees-Jones has been a member of the Fayed protection team since 1994, and as a former British soldier is held in high esteem for his discipline and military training.

In the course of the 30-minute journey the lovers bond in each others arms and look out at the wild Sardinian landscape. Dodi places a hand on Diana's thigh and she returns the gesture by placing hers in his lap.

They bask in the contentment of having known a landscape they are about to leave, but to which they plan to return as soon as possible. A Mercedes is their natural home when they are on the road, and both feel as comfortable in its interior, as they do in a hotel suite. They sustain a prolonged kiss, confident that Tomas Muzzi is every bit as discreet as his reputation has them believe.

The white Mercedes, together with a black companion car containing additional security, sweeps onto the apron of tarmac in front of the Gulfstream-IV jet which is waiting to fly the party to Paris. The couple board the aircraft, but unknown to them two photographers, Gavino Sanna and Luigi Folino, a freelance television cameraman, have found their way onto the platform of a Forklift truck and are positioned 30ft into the air in the attempt to make eye contact with Diana and Dodi.

Diana has come to represent the diverse talents of the modern woman to the media who she so avidly courts. She is the Cinderella of the Royal Family, the Lady of Shallot dreaming in her tower and imprisoned by protocol, and she is also the vulnerable divorcée intent on finding life again after a broken marriage. She is also loved for her rock'n'roll image and is compared to Madonna as the example of a celebrity who works out, and is financially independent. She is loved for being a passive victim and a charismatic saint to her charities. Unlike a time-warped Royal Family, she is prepared to air her vulnerabilities in public. Talking not just about her troubled marriage but about her eating disorder is an unprecedented move for a Royal. The Princess's popness is built not only on the art of her showmanship, but also on the appeal of her tactile qualities. She is a toucher and hugger and unashamedly so, always avoiding a tendency towards the mawkish by displaying emotions which are spontaneous and (seemingly) unrehearsed.

As the two Italian photographers zoom in on the couple as they take their seats on board the plane so they are aware of all the fantasy aspects of a woman who is regarded as an icon. The Princess is dressed in a beige trouser suit and her skin is flushed from the weeks spent on board the Jonikal. The couple snuggle together in the comfort of their seats, and at 1.24 p.m. the plane receives clearance to take off and four minutes later is in the air heading North towards Paris.

Unfortunately for the besieged lovers sipping champagne on their flight, news of their departure from Sardinia is already filtering through the paparazzi network. By the time the Gulfstream-IV jet lands at 3.20 p.m. at Le Bourget airport, 10 miles north of Paris, the paparazzi are crowding for shots of Diana while the tabloids are loud with the rumours that the couple may marry before the summer is out. The Princess's private life is the hottest media item on offer, and this time the assembled photographers intend to capture every public moment of the harassed couple's Paris sojourn. Dodi is seen in a protective role as he attempts to screen Diana from an over-zealous intrusion on the part of the paparazzi. He is coming to think of them as parasites. Anxious at first to soak up the full attention for the most publicised romance of the year, Dodi is becoming visibly irritated by the jackals who turn up everywhere.

"Bastards," he mutters, "they won't leave us alone." But Dodi, who is known to be impetuous, is not going to lose his cool. Dodi, a little resentful that his relationship with Diana is being commissioned by his father, Mohammed al Fayed the owner of Harrods, the London store, is nevertheless under the spell of the Princess's good looks. His father's powerful empire is in search of the right marriage to consolidate social foundations in Britain.

Meanwhile, staff at Le Bourget airport, renowned for its discreet cushioning of the glitterati from the press, have contacted the police about the great number of photographers' motorbikes propped up against the electronic perimeter gates. The new irreverent paparazzi, known as the "rats", are determined to run the couple into the ground. The idea that shedding light on the monarchy destroys its mystique is a theory trashed by a jackal pack finding Royalty a soap opera.

While the point of VIP aviation is to prevent celebrities being hounded by the press, there is nothing that Louis Demarque, a manager for Transair that handles arrivals at Le Bourget for the Ritz, can do about the menacing situation at hand.

He advises the couple to stay on the plane, until a police escort arrives to take them to the Bois de Boulogne. Diana remains calm and occasionally waves towards the cameras. Dodi is explosively angry at this confiscation of their privacy. He issues threats to senior ground staff who have boarded the plane, and complains loudly that confrontation with the press should have been avoided. Louis Demarque assures Dodi that he will do everything humanly possible to help the couple avoid the cameras, and to prevent their being followed in the Paris. Dodi explains that they don't have much time and are intending to fly out the next day, as Diana is due to return to Britain to see her sons, William and Harry, before the beginning of the new school term. The situation is tense and Dodi continues to demonstrate his displeasure at the mismanagement of the couple's arrival at Le Bourget. Diana does her best with the tension and assures Dodi that the fault doesn't lie with his father's staff. "I've become the most photographed person in the world darling, and you will have to get used to it," she sweet-talks into Dodi's ear. "Calm down, darling, or have another brandy."

Dodi instructs senior ground staff that he wants the waiting Fayed cars to drive to the bottom of the disembarkation steps. It is decided on board the plane that Trevor Rees-Jones is to be the first to disembark in an attempt to distract the photographers. Diana and Dodi brace themselves, receiving instructions to head straight for the black Mercedes waiting at the bottom of the steps and are told not to speak to waiting ground staff during their brief transit to the car. Rees-Jones hurries down the steps with the determined air of a man not to be messed with. There is a shout from the jackals as Diana appears, and contrary to warning, stops and greets the ground staff. She is full of smiles and is keyed up by the excitement of the situation. She has a word for every one, and seems in complete control of the situation. A few steps behind her, Dodi is abrupt and rankled. He is in the position of a man who is being forced to share his newly won lover with the world, and is impatient to conduct his romance with the Princess in the privacy of his apartment.

Parked alongside the black Mercedes is a dark green Range Rover being driven by Henri Paul, an assistant director of security at the Ritz. He is there as a support car to carry the couple's voluminous luggage.

Once the couple are in the safety of the limousine, Diana visibly relaxes, and smiles out of the window at the by now familiar rat-pack of photographers who have pursued her all summer. Diana's compulsion to attract more media attention than any other member of the Royal Family is peaking this summer, and for her it is a form of sweet revenge on an institution which has never felt comfortable with her PR campaign. Diana seems to be in competition with the Queen and her former husband in a conscious effort to have herself designated the People's Princess. Diana is confident that her relationship with Dodi is a romantic spectacular, and the press have every intention of capitalising on the event. That Dodi is a commoner adds fuel to public imagination, and Diana is clearly in the act of rebelling against her preconditioned class and status. She seems to be telling the Royal Family that they must either follow her example – and move with the times – or go.

More refined than the shambolic toe-sucked Fergie, Diana represents the modern woman streamlined to gain icon status. In her 1995 BBC Panorama interview Diana had voiced her wish "to be a Queen of people's hearts in people's hearts", and alluding to her by-then broken marriage with the Prince, she had expressed the opinion that she would remain popular, despite the unlikelihood of her ever becoming Queen. She had told her interviewer; "I don't think many people would want me to be Queen. Actually when I say 'people' I mean the Establishment that I married into because they have decided that I am a non-starter... because I do things differently, because I don't go by a rule book, because I lead from the heart, not the head. That's got me into trouble in my work, I understand that. But someone's got to go out there and love people and show it."

As Diana takes her place in the Mercedes she is once again, in the eyes of the establishment, breaking all the rules. She is richer by a divorce settlement believed to be around £15m, having originally asked for a sum in the region of £50m. Diana's too much too soon policy differs little from the material ambitions of her generation, although her wealth is small in comparison to pop stars like Elton John, Mick Jagger and David Bowie. If Princess Margaret had earned the wrath of the Royal Family decades earlier for rumours of an affair with Mick Jagger, then Diana is intent on maintaining this image by her relationship with the renowned playboy Fayed.

In the course of the car ride into Paris, Diana expresses a mother's natural concern over her two sons to the still prickly Dodi. Diana has not seen her children for a month, although she is consoled by William's telling her on the telephone in response to the media fuss over her relationship with Dodi, "Mummy I only want you to be happy." But Diana, who needs to feel guilty as her natural condition, is uneasy about the fact that her two sons have spent most of August at Balmoral with the Prince of Wales. Diana personally loathes this private home of the Royal Family cloaked in dense woodland, and rarely penetrated by the public. It reminds her of everything that is claustrophobic about the Queen and Charles. She has known appalling weeks there, thrown in with stuffy company, and with her heart yearning for the shopping sprees and stimulating company that London provides. She is worried too that Charles will use the occasion to influence the two boys in his favour. She can imagine Charles instructing them that their mother is a sensation-seeker on the prowl with a man unlikely to earn their respect.

Diana is anxious to tell Dodi all about her sons, as she wishes him to meet them on Monday. Dodi adjusts his dark sunglasses and stares meaningfully out of the car window as the Mercedes navigates the heavy holiday traffic before finally getting on to the motorway.

"Fire her up," Dodi advises the driver. "Get us there as though this traffic doesn't exist. Go, go, go." The driver blasts off, but not before a black Peugeot has the time to pull alongside and swerve in front of the Mercedes, and have Diana's car brake to a halt. This is a decoy to allow a motorbike to cut in close with the photographer riding pillion aiming his flash gun at Diana's side of the car. It's a cheeky manoeuvre on the photographer's part but no more than Diana has grown accustomed to.

The lovers are heading for a house that had been the home of the Duke and Duchess of Windsor after the war, and which is now in the ownership of Dodi's father Mohammed al Fayed. "Daddy bought it in 1987," Dodi tells Diana. "It was a bargain on a lease costing Fr.1m a year. I wish he'd picked up a few more of these places – we would be even richer."

Dodi appears to be lightening up, much to Diana's relief, and the couple hold hands in expectation of the pleasurable hours ahead. Dodi fills in Diana with more details about a house that they are considering making their own. "Daddy's refurbished the house," Dodi confides. "We are selling off 40,000 items from the house next month. Daddy says the sale will include an unpublished manuscript of a biography of the Duchess when she was Wallis Simpson."

Diana informs Dodi that she would like to have first option on this manuscript, for she is familiar with the story of how Wallis Simpson crossed France in the 1930s in the boot of a limousine to avoid photographers who were on her trail. Diana, who readily identifies with women in the role of victims in a male-structured society, feels affinities with Wallis Simpson, as she does with all women who undergo problem marriages.

When the Mercedes enters the drive and crunches up the gravel Diana can't contain her excitement. The couple rush into the house, and spend the next thirty minutes exploring the various floors. "It's wacky," they proclaim and would be ideal as a Paris hideaway. Diana's heart sinks when she realises that like Wallis Simpson she will never be Queen, but her spirits lift again at the thought of the superwealth that the couple will share. They are tempted to stay the night and sleep in the same bed as that shared by the Duke and Duchess of Windsor, but decide instead to head for the comfort of the Ritz. High on the excitement of summer romance, the two seem compelled to go direct to the heart of Paris, and to stay at the hotel which is another jewel in the Fayed empire.

The Mercedes drives into Paris, and enters the Place Vendome at exactly 4.35 p.m. The car stops majestically in front of the Ritz, and the couple are ushered into the foyer by the hotel's blue-jacketed doormen. To Dodi the Ritz is like home and his father has sent gifts and huge bouquets to greet the Princess. Dodi has entertained and bedded innumerable women at the sanctuary provided by his father, but this time, his gestures seem to imply, it's the big one. He exhibits the knowing wink of a well-seasoned voluptuary and directs staff to the couple's copious luggage.

Meanwhile the jackals who had invaded the couple's privacy on their arrival in Paris, are parking their motorbikes and taking up positions outside the hotel. They are used to this sort of game with celebrities, and a number of them are staking out the rear entrance, which leads on to the Rue Cambon. The rat pack are on familiar terms with the Ritz footmen, and pleasantries are exchanged by the two groups.

Inside the hotel, Diana and Dodi are taken straight to the Imperial Suite. A leading member of staff observes the couple fondling in the lift, with Dodi's hand reported to be on the Princess's backside. The Imperial Suite, a set of palatial chambers costing £6,000 a night, has been especially prepared for the couple. Vast quantities of flowers and an array of gifts sent from Harrods await the lovers. The suite is full of 18th century furniture, and chandeliers hang from a blue ceiling converging in a swathe of *trompe-l'oeil* clouds. Oil paintings adorn the cream-coloured walls. The couple have tasted the delights of the Imperial Suite on an earlier holiday, and quickly abandon themselves to its luxury. They intend to rest here for a while, before going on to Dodi's apartment. Diana touches up her face and undresses, while Dodi calls an old friend Hassan Yassin, a cousin of his mother's. Diana relaxes in a Janet Reger negligée, and calls her friend Richard Kay, a confidant and journalist on the Daily Mail. "I am super happy Richard," Diana purrs. "I'm thinking of giving it all up in November, and settling down with darling Dodos. I've had enough of the CC circus, and the flaming paps. You'll tell me if I'm doing right, won't you, Richard." Dodi finishes his call by informing Hassan Yassin that he and the Princess intend to marry very soon. As an afterthought he tells his friend about the pair of cufflinks that Diana has given him, an item of jewellery handed down to her from her late father, Earl Spencer. They are Dodi's pride and joy, and his father is eagerly awaiting the chance to view the heirlooms.

Diana settles at Dodi's side, and although she had appeared outwardly calm in the face of press harassment at the airport, she now gives voice to her frustration. She accuses the photographers staking out Kensington and her Health clubs of stalking and raping her. The advanced state of paranoia that had marked Diana's behaviour during her divorce settlement, is now unleashed on Dodi. Diana complains bitterly to Dodi of how her public role has been reduced as a result of her divorce. She tells

Dodi that although it's a curse being in the public eye, she wouldn't exchange it for anything. "I am going to win the landmine debate," she promises, "the Tory government are hopeless wimps, Dodos. We'll show them." Dodi has grown used to Diana's outbreaks, and takes her hand to calm her down. "You're much bigger than they are," he says. "Just think, they'd have you stag-shooting in Scotland, right now. You wanted to be the People's Queen, and that's what you are, darling."

Diana sips at a glass of champagne, and smiles into Dodi's eyes. The couple are bored, and anxious to get on to Dodi's Champs Elysées apartment. It's at this moment that Dodi decides to give Diana the ring he had ordered ten days previously from Alberto Repossi, a jeweller close to the hotel. Dodi is fond of giving his women jewellery, but this "friendship ring" has set him back a cool £130,000. Diana is thrilled by the ring and holds it up to the light as a gesture of appreciation. She places it over her heart before slipping it on to a finger for Dodi to admire. Dodi has chosen well, and Diana's mood switches to one of blissful happiness. The couple kiss deeply, and Diana tenderly wipes the lipstick smudges off Dodi's mouth.

The couple romance for a while, and vow complete devotion. Dodi brings up the question of marriage, but Diana is playful, and coyly talks round the subject. Dodi senses she may well say yes in the intimate surroundings of his apartment. He vows to himself to win Diana's hand that night. He has made a point of telling friends; "No more rubbers soon. We want kids."

They discuss the idea of having a quiet dinner at a discreet restaurant, Chez Benoit, in the busy 4th arrondissement near to the Pompidou Centre. The restaurant holds a Michelin star for its fine cuisine, and with a dinner for two costing as little as £150 it appears to the couple to offer an exclusive atmosphere conducive to intimate talk. A table is reserved for 8.45 p.m. in the name of the hotel manager at the Ritz.

The couple stay on in their Imperial Suite until the early evening. They are tired, and Dodi calls room service to have more champagne delivered to their suite. Even though they have decided not to spend the night at the Ritz, they continue to delight in the privacy that their rooms provide. Diana is beginning to dismantle her public image, and Dodi welcomes the motherly, benign woman who nestles in his arms on the sofa. Taking advantage of Diana's mellowing mood, Dodi presents her with a box of sleazy knickers purchased at Agent Provocateur.

The couple leave the hotel at 6.40 and are driven in a black Mercedes to Dodi's Etoile flat at 1 Rue Arsene Houssaye, arriving there at exactly 7.15 p.m. The flat commands a panoramic view of Paris, taking in the Place de la Concorde in one direction, and in the other the Arc de Triomphe. The black Mercedes is once again followed by the back-up dark green Range Rover, and despite the hassle of changing residences, the couple appear to be in good spirits. Bodyguards jump out of the car on arrival at Rue Arsene Houssaye and disperse the paparazzi who have anticipated the couple's plans. It's not expected that the couple will return to the Ritz that night, and Henri Paul as acting head of security makes final checks on the arrangements for Diana's flight to Britain the following day. Henri Paul is a friend of Dodi's, as well as a highly regarded security officer, who sometimes goes out for dinner with his employer. Henri Paul is confident that his services will not be required again that night, and relaxes with the knowledge that the couple are safely ensconced in Dodi's spectacular second-floor apartment. Henri Paul is known as a reliable and faithful employee of the Fayeds, and has rapidly won promotion from being employed on temporary contracts to being retained as one of Dodi's personal security team on a salary of £25,000 per annum. He is a quiet man, and is known as ultra-competent to his fellow employees, and is valued by the Fayeds as an indispensable member of staff. He is known to drink in gay bars, but pursues what is said to be a straight lifestyle. Paul leaves the Ritz at 7.05 p.m. in his black Mini, and does not expect to be on duty again that evening. His dedication to work will have him respond to a call from the Ritz later that night to chauffeur the couple on their last ill-fated journey.

Inside Dodi's flat the couple have abandoned ideas of dining at the Benoit restaurant. Security officers have informed Dodi that the rat pack are waiting outside in the Champs Elysées. The couple are advised that they will meet with little privacy at the Benoit, and that the Ritz is better able to provide the intimacy for the sort of dinner they have planned. Their reservation at Benoit is duly cancelled, and the couple linger in loving embraces before getting changed for dinner. Time alone is crucial to them, and they hold on to the togetherness that the privacy of Dodi's apartment provides. "Now that I've found you, don't ever leave me Dodos," Diana murmurs, as she strokes her lover's chest. "This is my best summer ever," Dodi responds. "I never dreamed I would meet a woman like you." "You're my hottest lover," says Diana.

Diana looks at the friendship ring again, and knows that a proposal is not far away. "I may have a very special question to ask you over dinner, darling," Dodi grins. "I've been waiting for it ever since I set eyes on you," Diana whispers. The couple kiss and look deep into each other's eyes. "I see my future in your eyes," says Dodi; "and mine in yours," replies Diana. "Oh darling!"

Half an hour later at 9.30 p.m. the couple leave the apartment for what will tragically be the last time. Dodi is wearing cowboy boots, blue jeans, a light grey shirt and a brown jacket. Diana is in white slacks and a black top and jacket.

The black Mercedes begins its journey through sluggish traffic in the direction of the Ritz. Dodi is always impatient with delay, and tells his driver to beat the traffic. "Lets go for it," he says, and Diana squeezes his hand. The rats are in hot pursuit, but the Mercedes is too powerful for them. "Bastards," Diana groans, and the couple take delight in their superior vehicle. Dodi and Diana are in high spirits, and they promise the driver a bottle of champagne if he gets them to the Ritz double quick. The driver looks at the pursuing rat-pack in his mirror and says, "They're scum, Mr Fayed. We'll be at the Ritz in no time, Sir."

At 9.52 p.m., according to the Ritz security cameras, the Mercedes enters the square in front of the hotel. Staff struggle with a gypsy woman, who is trying to break through the ranks of photographers. The woman is shouting "Beware of that car. Don't use that car Ma'am. Beware."

The woman, who is considered to be a nutter, is pushed back and told to shut up. Her voice is drowned out by the press, who are trying to attract Diana's attention. By now nearly 50 photographers are milling around outside.

A line of security men is resisting the efforts of the jackals to push forward, but the latter have succeeded in getting within 10 yards of the hotel steps. The mood has grown tense, and the rats are doing their best to wind security staff up. The earlier cordial relations between staff and media are starting to turn sour, and mobile telephones are going off everywhere. The press are anxious to meet their tabloid deadlines, which are set at midnight for tomorrow's dailies. There are minor skirmishes, as they jostle for places. Unfortunately for Diana and Dodi another car is unloading in front of them, and they are forced to wait. The rat pack pushes forward and blitzes the Mercedes with flashes. The couple are defenceless against this intrusion. Their romance is being converted into money with every flash, and Diana is once again the world's leading media exhibit. She tells Dodi that Charles was right when he had called the Royal Family a soap opera. "It's worse for me," she tells Dodi, "as I am the only glamorous one."

The couple briefly remain in the car, holding each other's hands for support, and at a signal scurry into the hotel. They show signs of concern and amusement at their having become in the space of a month the world's biggest romance.

Inside the hotel, the couple walk briefly through the Espadon restaurant. The undue attention given them by the restaurant's diners has them decide to have dinner in their Imperial Suite. Diana is fast realising that the decision to return to the Ritz has been a wrong one. The couple agree that they should have stayed at Dodi's apartment, and had the Ritz or the Benoit send over dinner to the flat. Dodi's private staff would have provided expert catering, and their spirit of romance would have continued uninterrupted. The couple are not worried about their personal safety, and are quickly resigned to the luxury that the Imperial Suite bestows on them. Dodi and Diana relax in comfort and pick at the dishes that Dodi has personally requested. They take their time and Dodi tells the Princess that a dessert of champagne and cocaine will prove to be a powerful intoxicant. They have so much to tell each other. Diana pours out her heart over her broken marriage and the series of snubs given her by the royal family. As a deeply maternal, loving woman, Diana's concerns are always those of her two sons. She tells Dodi, perhaps scenting a proposal, that Charles' heart is so totally with Camilla Parker Bowles, that the boys would benefit from having a father whose public duties are less arduous. Charles is always away on public engagements, or is holidaying with friends in the countryside, or isolating himself at Highgrove, Diana explains. The boys need a father figure in their lives who is not so removed. She fears that Harry and William will grow up as the products of a broken marriage, and suffer from the same feelings of being unwanted as their mother. An interested father figure, Diana confirms, would swing things round in the boys' favour. They would have someone to look up to and call Daddy. "They need a strong man to help them through their education," the Princess declares.

Dodi has been longing to hear Diana place this ball in his court, and he rises to the situation with suitable charm. "We could do this together," he whispers, already imagining the rewards he will reap from his father. Dodi backs up Diana's conviction that her boys need a regular father, and lying back, the very picture of hirsute masculinity, he takes Diana in his arms and assures her that their future together will be a golden one. Lacking children of his own is an additional incentive to begin an old and new family, he tells the Princess. Diana would like two girls, and Dodi promises to oblige. He has, he says, all the makings of a good father. "I am your devoted Dodi for ever," he tells the flushed Diana. Dodi pours a particularly fine Chablis, and the couple dream of a long future together.

It's at this point – according to the author's transcription tapes, for the Imperial

Suite was expertly bugged – that Dodi proposes to Diana. "I speak for myself Diana in saying that I have never known or ever will again such love for a woman. I would like to ask for your hand in marriage." There's a pause in which Diana goes silent, an over-extended pause in which Dodi can be heard pouring another drink, before she joyously says, "Yes. Dodi Fayed, I give you my hand in marriage."

The couple have expressed a wish to return to Dodi's apartment later that night, and their security team know that if they are going to get them out of the hotel without incident it will require ingenious thinking. At 9.50 p.m. the Ritz call the greatly respected Henri Paul at home. They tell him that Dodi and Diana wish to return to Rue Arsene Hussaye tonight, and that he is to be their trusted driver. Paul, who is perfectly steady on his feet, parks his black Mini in a side street and walks through the aggressive crowd into the Ritz. On entering the hotel he turns left from the hall and joins Rees-Jones and Wingfield, another bodyguard, at the bar. The two Britons are enjoying a snack and Paul, having got a pineapple juice at the bar, joins them. The three of them engage in gossip surrounding Dodi and Diana's relationship, and go on to speak a little about their personal lives. Rees-Jones and Wingfield confess to being lonely on tour, and although the pay is good they long to be back home. "I live alone," Paul says in his Anglo-French accent, "and it's easier that way. I can come out at any time for the boss." The three security staff amuse each other with anecdotes relating to their work.

They have all been witnesses to the private lives of the big timers. A transcription tape has Paul telling the other two of a time when he had chauffeured Dodi across Paris at night, and his boss had taken the dress off his date in the car. To the amusement of the others, Henri Paul describes the bumpy ride home across the city "It was hard to keep the car on the road," he laughs over his third grapefruit juice.

As the couple are still intent on spending the night in the apartment on the Champs Elysées, it is agreed amongst the bodyguards that the only discreet way out of the hotel is through the rear entrance, along the narrow Rue Cambon. They are all familiar with a route that Paul has taken often in the needs of discretion for the Al Fayeds. As the plans take shape Paul comes up with an idea to shake off the paparazzi. He will pick up the couple at the back of the hotel in a limousine and take off on the fast road on the north bank of the Seine. If his plan succeeds the Mercedes will get far enough away from the chasing jackals to allow a quick turn into the 16th arrondissement without being seen by them. Paul estimates that it will then prove easy work to negotiate the back streets without being followed and drop the couple off outside Dodi's flat. He hopes by this strategy to fool the paparazzi into the belief that the couple are to spend the night at the Windsor House in the Bois de Boulogne. Paul jokes with staff at the Ritz about the prospects of his scheme establishing a false chase across Paris. Paul is still drinking fruit juices and at no time gives any indication of being unsteady or drunk. His organisational capacities are as proficient as ever, and Rees-Jones and Wingfield give their full approval to the scheme he has devised. Paul goes one step further in his plan, and arranges a decoy system outside in the hotel's front square. Paul instructs staff to have a substitute black Mercedes parked at the hotel's entrance, together with the green Range Rover used earlier to carry the couple's baggage. Two additional cars are enlisted as part of the decoy strategy, and Paul arranges to have footmen regularly go out to the vehicles and appear to be preparing them for departure. The rat pack are told on several occasions that they have only ten minutes to wait, and each time the by now restless crowd grows excited. Time equals big money for the photographers who stalk Diana, and for many of them their tabloid deadlines are running out. They are growing suspicious of the indications given to them by the Ritz security staff, and about ten of the jackals have decided to risk it, and hang out at the back of the hotel. They park their Hondas in the Rue Cambon prepared to give chase should the couple leave by the hotel's rear entrance. Some of the photographers like Christian Martinez and Jacques Langevin are noted as masters of intrusive photography. They are known to work with the stealth of assassins when in pursuit of their quarry, but Langevin is tired of waiting and decides to call it a day. He believes that the couple will remain at the Ritz all night, and clears off, in his Volkswagen Golf. But not so his colleagues, who sense that they are still in with a chance to sell to the British tabloids. They have all known this sort of situation before, and feel that Diana is playing for time, in order to make a secret getaway. The rat pack fan out to cover the hotel and the nearby streets.

Meanwhile in the Imperial Suite Diana and Dodi are discussing their recent visit to the clairvoyant, Rita Rogers. Diana is chuckling over the large pink sofa on which they had sat facing Rita, and both had liked the way in which she had treated them as no different from her other clients. "What impressed me," says Diana "is the way the temperature dropped. Do you remember how icy it became, when Rita talked of the future. God the shivers that ran down my spine." Dodi, who is a natural sceptic of the spiritual world, recollects the temperature drop, and the light that had come into Rita's face at the time. "It freaked me out for days," Diana adds, while Dodi sinks deeper into the cushions.

"Some of it was a bit scary," Diana continues. "I don't know what Rita meant by a catastrophe." "Probably something to do with the millennium," Dodi replies. "You get all that shit at the end of the century."

Dodi at this point of the conversation tells Diana that he feels they lack adequate security. His father, Dodi relates, travels in an armoured Mercedes 600 with a back-up car full of medical equipment to be used in case of emergency. His security staff work in teams of five at a time, whereas he and Diana have been allocated a simple bodyguard. Dodi complains that their Mercedes is not armoured, and that his father always treats him as an inferior. "But you shouldn't have been scared, when we drove in from the airport today," he tells Diana. "My first car was a red Ferrari Testarossa. I've always loved speed. You've got to get used to the thrill of it."

It's known to the police that earlier in the day Diana had repeatedly asked the driver to slow down, when the couple were driven from Le Bourget to the Windsor house. She had expressed fears of an accident, or of the car dislodging a motorcycle photographer. She remembers Dodi smiling, and encouraging the driver to keep his foot down on the accelerator. Dodi's machismo takes pleasure in fast cars and boats, and in the fact that nobody ever dares disobey the Al Fayed organisation. "One wrong move and you're out," is what Mohammed has taught his son to tell staff in his employ.

The couple are not anxious to directly leave their rooms. Dodi gets a perverse pleasure out of winding up the press, and knows that the longer they are made to wait the less likelihood there is of their getting photos in the British Sundays. Dodi still resents a photograph called "The Kiss" which had been the beginning of the whole cycle of paparazzi activity. An Italian Mario Brenna had managed to sneak a shot of the couple kissing on board the Fayed yacht. Even though the photograph was shot from a quarter of a mile off Sardinia, Dodi has been informed that the Sunday Mirror paid £250,000 for first rights in Britain. The Sun and the Mail had paid another £100,000 each to run the shot again the next day. There had also been shots bought by the Mail of Diana indecorously swinging a leg over Dodi, on the pillion of a jet-ski. Photographers had boasted to the media that they were always twelve hours ahead of the romancing couple, and were waiting for them before the couple reached their destination.

Dodi warns Diana that one of the unusual features of his father's hotel, the Paris Ritz, is that the suites can be bugged. Dodi warns Diana that his father's security staff have secretly filmed and recorded guests in the hotel using secret cameras and microphones. Dodi confides to Diana that his father has spent £40 million in refurbishing the Ritz, and the place is a private hobby of his. The Ritz isn't run at a profit, Dodi boasts. It is the Fayed's private fiefdom, he proudly continues, and tells Diana that one day he will be its owner. "We'll sell the place, and reap hay," he says.

Henri Paul is meanwhile tightening existing security arrangements. He calls through to his boss in the Imperial Suite to inform him that the car is ready at the hotel's rear. It's 11.45 p.m. when Paul makes this call to Dodi, but again Diana plays for time. She has been shocked by the earlier skirmishes with the rats, and tries to persuade Dodi into staying the night at the Ritz. "The bed here is fabulous," Diana protests, but Dodi claims his Champs Elysées apartment offers greater privacy. Dodi is apprehensive that his father may have bugged the Imperial Suite. Dodi lives in his father's shadow, and knows that the latter is disappointed over his failure to meet with a purpose in life. Dodi has irritated his father by resigning from the director's post created for him at Harrods, and by continuing to live as a dependent playboy. Dodi knows only too well that his father will not be pleased at having to foot the bill for Diana's £130,000 engagement ring.

Diana's mind is still on the subject of seeing her children the next day. The fact that Charles is to be a part of the get-together has her instantly feel crest-fallen. She raises the subject of taking Dodi with her, as a snub to Charles. Diana is imagining Charles' face when he is confronted by her Muslim boyfriend. "It'll cause a crashing stir darling," she tells Dodi. "But I'm worried about my cellulite. The press are on to it. Is it bad on my thighs?"

Henri Paul is still attending to security. He is a naturally anxious individual, and his job entails high stress. He is responsible for sacking incompetent members of staff, and it goes against the grain for him to have to create enemies in this way. Paul, who is from Lorient in Brittany, is known as a solitary person, who likes to drink in his off-duty hours. For two years, until 1995, he had shared his apartment with Laurence Pujol, a woman ten years his junior, and her daughter Samantha. When Laurence had ended their relationship, Paul had gone through a crisis, but had never allowed it to interfere with his work at the Ritz. Dodi had proved sympathetic to Paul's problems, and had on occasions taken him out to dinner. Paul's drinking places are local ones like Le Bourgogne, Le Mazarin, Willi's Wine Bar and Bazin's. He is someone known to pace his drinks, and attaches great responsibility to his job. He has never reported for duty drunk, nor has the suspicion ever arisen in the course of his enjoyment that he is a danger on the road. Paul keeps himself to himself and is the ideal Fayed's employee. A man who is loyal, discreet, and who jumps to it when ordered. The Fayeds have no hesitation in sacking underachievers, and Paul is considered to be a valuable employee.

Unknown to the Ritz, Paul is being prescribed two anti-depressant drugs, Prozac and Triapide. As he runs up and down stairs in trainers, checking on security relations, he feels jaunty and grateful to Dodi that he has trusted him with the job. He's had some wine earlier on at home, but not enough to make him feel good.

Paul has been advised by his doctor

not to mix drink and drugs, but like most people he finds he can combine the two without noticeable effects. He's used to combining the two now, and doesn't even give it a thought. He's generally in good health, and apart from bouts of depression, considers himself to be healthy. His work is his life, and he's proud to be attached to the Ritz security staff. He has a taste for Ricard and Bourbon, and promises himself that after dropping the couple off at Dodi's flat, he'll have a few stiff drinks at home. He likes drinking at the hotel as the barmen are generous with measures, but he abstains tonight as he's on duty. For Paul it's a routine journey, and he knows at heart that the press are excitable, but only doing their duty. He knows also that by following his master plan, he will burn off the rat pack and get the couple home in fifteen minutes. He knows very well that no-one has ever been killed by a photographer's flash, and that all he is really protecting is the couple's request for privacy. He's used to the sort of canoodling his employer gets up to in cars, and just wants to get the job over and go home.

Dodi telephones to tell Paul that the couple will be down and ready to leave at 12.15 a.m. The decoy cars are to take off around the square in front of the hotel, while the couple escape from the rear. Dodi is in high spirits as the Princess has accepted his proposal, and Paul is humoured by knowing that his employer has been drinking. Paul knows when things are going well with Dodi, and knows that he will be well rewarded for his work.

Paul knows he has to drag out another ten minutes of waiting, and tapes from the Imperial Suite record a silence, as the couple share passionate kisses. There are deep sighs and moans and murmured declarations of love. It's obvious from Diana's part that she doesn't want to leave, and she encourages Dodi to join her in the bedroom. Dodi tells the Princess that it's important they go back to his apartment, as he has several big surprises waiting in store for her there. "A very big surprise," he jokes.

Paul jogs upstairs to the Imperial Suite to give Dodi the word that they are set to go. He knocks three times, and Dodi appears at the door. Paul, who comes from a simple childhood, never ceases to wonder at the huge fuss that celebrities make over having a few pictures taken. Tonight according to other members of security is not very different from any other. Diana is always mobbed by the press and demands their attention. One member of staff has bluntly referred to Diana's attitude as the pot calling the kettle black. Why Diana is so nervous tonight no-one properly understands. Some members of staff attribute it to her insecurity in being without her own bodyguards, and others put it down to her unhappiness at having to end her holiday for the kids.

Paul is keyed up to go, and as Prozac is largely an alcohol-resistant drug, he's feeling good about himself, and ready to chauffeur his distinguished passenger to Dodi's flat. Paul likes to name-drop, and driving Diana is a welcome acquisition to the list of celebrities with whom he has come in contact during his Ritz employment. Diana and Dodi are taken by security staff to the hotel's entrance. At 12.21 the decoy is put into action. The green Range Rover in front of the hotel, together with a substitute Mercedes, take off hard into the Place Vendôme. The milling paparazzi fire off a burst of flashes and run for their bikes. The cars, however, much to the photographers frustration, merely drive once around the square and return to their former parking spaces.

"Let's go for it," Rees-Jones shouts, and Dodi guides Diana out of the back of the Ritz and into the waiting limousine. It's 12.20. Rees-Jones takes up his position in the front passenger seat next to Paul, and Diana and Dodi occupy the car's rear seat.

There are a few paparazzi waiting near the rear of the hotel, and Paul playfully jokes out the window, "You'll not catch me this time."

Paul burns the Mercedes along the Rue de Rivoli, and screeches into the Place de la Concorde. Dodi, who loves fast driving, watches Rees-Jones instinctually fasten his seatbelt. Paul tells Dodi that he's aiming for the quais, a two-lane expressway parallel with the right bank of the Seine, then through the Alma tunnel to the western edge of Paris. Paul knows that Dodi will welcome the burn-out along a fast straight road. The Mercedes 280-S is equipped with three-point rear seat harnesses, but neither Dodi nor Diana make use of their seat belts. Rees-Jones apparently fails to alert the couple to what should be straightforward procedure. Paul builds the car to 60 m.p.h. in the Place de la Concorde, but is pulled up by a red traffic light at the junction with the Champs Elysées. The chasing paparazzi catch up with the car at this point, and one of them, Romuald Rat uses his cellphone to call ahead to colleagues that Diana and Dodi are on their way to the Etoile flat.

Anxious to outdistance the paparazzi, Paul jumps the lights before they turn green, and clocks up 90 m.p.h. as he swings the Mercedes right on to the quai. The paparazzi chase in hot pursuit, but theirs is a losing game. Despite the fact they build to 60 m.p.h. along the quai, they are not even in view of the Mercedes' tail lights. Paul is carrying out his boast about not intending to be caught with exemplary panache. He pushes the Mercedes to a speed of about 110 m.p.h. along the straight as an approach to the Alma tunnel. Paul is no stranger to the Alma tunnel, nor to approaching it at high speed. The tunnel, as he knows, forms part of the expressway along the right bank of the Seine opposite the Eiffel Tower. It's a Paris landmark and is supported by 15ft tall, reinforced concrete pillars. Paul knows from regular acquaintance with the tunnel, that there's a curve at the entrance followed by a dip. It's not an entrance to take at high speed, but this time for the sheer hell of it, he will risk blazing through.

Paul checks his mirror to see that he has successfully outstripped the rat-pack, and notices a limousine behind him has appeared on the Cours Albert Ier towards the tunnel. He congratulates himself on having left the press behind, and hurtles the car towards the entrance of the Alma Tunnel. At this point, the car swings violently out of control. Paul hears the impact against the tunnel's right wall, then the car ricochets diagonally 15 metres across the road, mounts the curb and smashes face-on into the thirteenth pillar, spins round and comes to rest facing the wrong way, its horn blaring. Paul, who is directly in the line of impact, dies immediately as the bonnet caves in, and the engine is rammed back through the car. The massive head-on impact kills Dodi outright, and he is thrown distortedly sideways. The front passenger door on Rees-Jones' side has been ripped off, and his upper body hangs out of the car. He is unconscious, and bleeding profusely. The Princess, who drifts in and out of consciousness, finds herself trapped in the well between the front and rear seats. Her legs have buckled under her, and in a half kneeling position she has been projected forward so that her chin is pressed tightly against her chest. She appears to be without external injuries, and her face is unscarred. The car's airbags have failed to inflate, due to the high speed collision, as have its protective 'crumple zones'. The force of impact has rendered useless the limousine's 'safety cell' designed to protect passengers in head-on collisions. The Mercedes, chosen for its being one of the safest cars in the world has ended up with its radiator in the driver's foot well, so ferocious has been the crash impact.

When Rat arrives on his bike a minute later, he opens the rear door and feels Diana's neck for a pulse. Speaking to her in broken English he assures her that help is at hand. The whole rat-pack have arrived by now and are shooting flashes at the victims of the catastrophe.

As luck has it, a white Ford Fiesta approaching from the opposite direction, contains Dr. Frederic Mailliez, who works for SOS Medecins, an emergency callout service. Realising there has been a serious crash, he stops his car and hurries over to help. A French doctor in his mid-thirties, Mailliez is used to this sort of work, and recognizes immediately that two of the passengers are almost certainly dead. Seeing that the man in the front passenger seat, and the blonde woman in the rear of the car are still alive, he runs back to his car for oxygen masks and to telephone emergency services. It's 12.26 a.m., and the car horn continues to remain jammed. Dr. Mailliez manages to fit an oxygen mask to Diana, and to lift her head back from her chest, so that she can breathe more freely. The paparazzi are firing shots at the victims and at the wrecked car, but in no way impede Dr. Mailliez's work. The car, which has come to a halt in 46 thousandths of a second, generating a force of 70g, is an atrocity exhibit to the untiringly rapacious press. As Mailliez succeeds in forcing Diana's head back to free the air passage, he can hear the over-excited photographers shouting to him, "speak to her in English." Mailliez is unaware that the woman trapped in the concertinaed car is Princess Diana, and hears her groaning and mumbling incoherently.

Two of the identifiable rat-pack, Arsov and Langevin, manage to take close-up pictures, while the police set up a cordon to keep onlookers away. By 12.30 the police have succeeded in blocking off the two west-bound lanes of the tunnel. There are photographers kneeling around the back right-hand side of the Mercedes where the door is flung open. The police have called for back-up and emergency medical teams as a support to Dr. Mailliez's earlier request and estimate of injuries. Two Japanese tourists are staring at the accident site, and have entered the central reservation, while photographers are in heated discussion with the police. They argue that they are only doing their duty, and are reporting on the crash. Three of the paparazzi get away after shooting rolls of film, and still no ambulance has arrived on the scene.

By 12.40 a.m. three fire engines and

the same number of mobile resuscitation units arrive to relieve Mailliez. The firemen slice off the top of the car with electric chain saws and set about freeing Rees-Jones and Diana from the vehicle. Diana, who is losing blood from internal injuries, is given a transfusion on site. Her pulse is weak, and the resuscitation team at La Pitié Saltpêtrière hospital are alerted that Princess Diana's condition is critical, and that they are to gown up and enter the operating theatre to await her arrival. Professor Bruno Riou, Professor Pierre Loriat, head of anaesthetics, Professor Alain Pavie, a chest and heart surgeon, and Professor Jean-Pierre Bénazet, supported by four senior nurses and four other surgical staff are in the theatre within minutes, and listen to information relayed to them by paramedics on the scene. They are told that Diana is unconscious, and has shown no response to external heart massage, and has suffered a massive heart attack.

At 1.55 a.m. the team receive a message saying that the ambulance carrying Diana has set off from the tunnel. It has taken so long to free her from the car, that the medical team are doubtful she will arrive at the hospital alive. A second ambulance carrying Rees-Jones leaves the tunnel at 1.59 a.m.

At precisely 2 a.m., the ambulance carrying Diana, enters the hospital's main gate, and she is rushed to the operating theatre. Professor Riou opens Diana's chest to discover that the cavity surrounding her left lung has been flooded by blood from a lesion in the vein connecting the heart and lungs. With Diana's blood pressure critically low, Riou and Pavie locate the tear in the pulmonary vein, and begin the repair. But Diana's heart fails to respond to hand massage or to drugs or electric shocks to kick-start the heart. By 3.45 a.m. Riou stitches up the chest cavity and pronounces Diana dead. There is nothing more that he and his colleagues can do, despite the extraordinary attempts they have made to have the Princess live. After having closed the cavity, Riou notices that Diana has lost one of her pearl earrings in a dish. Later, the director of the hospital Thierry Merresse will say, "The surgeons went far beyond the bounds of duty, far beyond anything that has been done before. It was a superhuman effort on their part."

It was all over. Some of the nurses

broke down in tears, while the surgeons who had heroically worked for almost two hours to restore Diana's life felt an overwhelming sense of failure.

Meanwhile, the police who had arrested seven photographers in the Alma Tunnel, were strip-searching the men at their Quai des Orfévres headquarters, in the hope of confiscating photographs taken of the crash. The photographers, including the notorious Rat are held for further questioning, and are taken to the cells.

Romuald Rat's part in the affair remains ambiguous. He claims to have gone to Diana's assistance immediately, on arriving at the wrecked car. On his own evidence he claims to have pulled the rear door open on Diana's side, and to have found her trapped between the front and back seats. He informs the police that he lifted her head in order to see if she was still alive, and told her in English that an ambulance was on the way. Rat claimed that he then went to Rees-Jones' assistance, and discovered that the latter was alive. He claims that he only began to shoot film after the emergency services arrived. According to Stéphane Darmon, a courier for the Gamma picture agency in Paris, who was employed on the fateful night of the crash by Romuald Rat, and also detained by police, there was an argument amongst the first of the rats to arrive at the scene. "There were 10 or 15 photographers and maybe some onlookers. Romuald opened the rear righthand door. Serge Arnal from Stills made a sign to indicate he was calling the emergency services. Some police officers arrived. There was a row between them and I only saw it from a distance... Romuald opened the car door to try to help. He has a first-aid certificate. You could say he is used to seeing horrible things but then, look at me, I just stood there, petrified with horror."

While the photographers are being questioned by the police, who are intent on charging them with manslaughter and a failure to help victims of an accident, excitement floods a photo agency in the Rue Flatters. Two of the photographers employed by the Laurent Sola agency have managed to escape from the tunnel with 30 or 40 photographs taken at the accident site. There are copious shots of the smashed Mercedes and of Dodi's body that had been pulled out of the car and onto the ground, in the hopes of filming signs of life in his body. But immediate examination of the photos showed a number of pictures of Diana still alive in the car. One of the photographs was a clear shot of the Princess's face, a hand stretched out as if reaching for Dodi. Sola knows that the photographs are worth a fortune on the international market, but withdraws the pictures from sale, once he knows the Princess is dead.

Confirmation of Diana's being conscious after the ferocity of the collision was given by Sebastien Dorzee, the first policeman to arrive in the tunnel. According to Dorzee's account, "The Princess had turned round in relation to her initial sitting position and her head was between the two seats and she could see Dodi's dead body in front of her. Her eyes were open as she moved, talking to me in English. When she saw her friend was dead, I think she said, 'My God.' At the same time she rubbed her stomach. She was in pain." Dorzee also states that the Princess noted the driver was dead, and kept feeling around her, and saying incoherent things. Other close-up witnesses will claim that Diana asked to be left alone, before she lapsed into unconsciousness. That it took emergency services an hour to cut through the heavy-duty vehicle in order to remove Diana from her trapped position in the car counted heavily against her chances of survival. If the Princess had been wearing a seatbelt, it is estimated by experts that she would like Rees-Jones have survived. She would have suffered fractured ribs and shoulders, and have incurred internal injuries, but her condition would not have been fatal.

News that Diana is inside La Pitié Salpêtrière hospital, has brought the paparazzi in large numbers to the building's precincts. Some of them have gained entrance to neighbouring houses and have bribed the occupants to let them take up position on surrounding balconies and rooftops. To ensure maximum security the staff inside the hospital clear the first floor, have it staffed by police guards, and add blackout sheets to the blinds or the windows. Diana's body is guarded by security, who will not leave her side. The nurses are delighted to discover that the Princess's face remains unscarred, and that her beauty remains even in death. She is still wearing a number of the bracelets she had selected for her Paris trip, together with a number of rings dear to her. A number of the nursing staff will later comment on how peaceful Diana looked in death, and of their being no external evidence that she had been involved in the most appalling collision. She appeared serene and untouched by the catastrophe she has encountered.

At Balmoral, the royal residence that Diana so despised, Charles has been woken and informed of the catastrophe. News has reached Charles through Sir Michael Jay, the British ambassador in Paris having telephoned Robin Janvrin, the Queen's deputy private secretary. It is Janvrin who breaks the news to the Prince, who sits up listening to the radio for information. It is still uncertain amongst conflicting media sources if Diana is actually dead or seriously injured. No official announcement has been made, and Charles after speaking to his mother and Camilla Parker Bowles, decides not to impart the news to his sons until the morning. Some of the British tabloids will go to press reporting that Diana is still alive, although critically injured. They will carry headlines Dodi Dead, Diana Injured, and much of the British populace will on first reading the news entertain the hope that Diana has survived the crash.

Charles is not told of Diana's death until 3 a.m. (British time), and feels it best to leave the boys undisturbed. Diana's two sisters, Lady Jane Fellowes and Lady Sarah McCorquodale are also informed of the tragedy, and are later to fly to Aberdeen, where Charles joined the plane, en route for Paris.

But another mysterious call is made to Marie Bijou at 2.10 a.m. to tell her of

Dodi and Diana's deaths. Marie had been out earlier that night with her then boyfriend, Henri Montesquiou, and had only just returned to her flat in the Champs Elysées. She is aware that there has been an accident, as the car driving her home has been diverted from the Alma underpass to another route. It's just another accident, one of the hundreds that occur in Paris each year. When Marie gets into bed, she is awoken by an unidentified caller who tells her the hot news. She is told that Dodi Fayed is dead, and that she is never to talk about her relationship with him, because of the involvement with Princess Diana. She is never to make public the fact that her relationship with Dodi has existed at the same time as his involvement with the Princess. Marie is told that she has a reservation on a flight to Connecticut at 8.20 p.m. on Sunday. Money is provided and funds await her on arrival in America. She is told that everything will be taken care of. Marie is shocked, but has no alternative but to agree to leave Paris for a time specified as six months. The money is to be paid on the condition that she doesn't talk. She is never again permitted to speak of her affair with Dodi.

By 10 a.m., Diana's personal valet has arrived in Paris, carrying a small suitcase containing her clothes and make-up. He is driven to the hospital, and begins to prepare her body. With the lightness of touch that accompanies a solemn ritual, he dresses the corpse in a simple black cocktail dress, coming to just below the knee. He has chosen perfectly, for the dress compliments the sobriety of the occasion, while serving to enhance Diana's beauty in death. It is a wrap-around dress with long sleeves and a collar and a belt of the same material. The dress has been cut to form a V-neck where it crosses at the front. The valet spends a long time applying Diana's make-up, knowing that this will be the last time ever that he performs this function. He is sad, dignified and patient as he works on her dead face. He creates in her the natural look adored by the crowds, this woman who has rightly described herself as the Queen of Hearts is to be made to look beautiful to the end. The valet completes his work, and says a short prayer for the Princess. He looks at her face and seems satisfied that he has got it as true to life as is possible. Only then does he leave the room in the intensive care unit, and go outside to his waiting car. His job, the most unexpected and important of his life is done.

As a bizarre episode in the chain of events, Charles is informed on board his BAe 146 aircraft of the Royal Squadron, that as Diana was no longer a member of the royal family, her body is to be transported to Fulham mortuary. This is standard procedure. Charles expresses his views that any such move would be inadvisable and would lead to a national scandal. Charles speaks to Sir Michael Jay, the British ambassador in Paris, then to the Queen, and to a network of contacts until it is agreed that her body is to be brought back to St James' Palace in London. "Don't lose your cool darling," Camilla tells Charles, shortly before the royal plane arrives at 5 p.m. at

Villacoublay, a military airfield situated to the southwest of Paris. Charles and Diana's two sisters are quickly ushered to the hospital where they are awaited by President Jacques Chirac. "I understand there's been a spot of trouble," Charles says to Chirac by way of greeting, as the party walk towards the intensive care unit. Charles and Diana's two sisters are taken to Diana's bed by the Rev Martin Draper, from the Anglican cathedral in Paris.

Diana's body has already been prepared and placed in a coffin, and Charles is given the option of looking on the body or not. He declines, but stays at the coffin's side for a number of minutes, before meeting the four surgeons and four nurses who had battled so valiantly to save the Princess. Charles talks to the anaesthetist Bruno Riou, and to Alain Pavie, the thoracic and cardiac surgeon who had tended to Diana. Pierre Coriat, head of the hospital anaesthetic unit, and Professor Jean Pierre Benazet are also in attendance to offer condolences. "Quel jour; quelle horreur," one of them remarks to the Prince.

Charles, who appears to be deeply moved, regains his composure, and reflects on the turbulent years that have brought his former wife to a premature grave. Although it is thought that Charles never truly loved Diana, her death is still a shattering blow to his life. Diana's £15m divorce settlement, and the publicity campaign she had staged over the proceedings had brought their estranged lives to a bitter conclusion, but Charles still feels love for the mother of his children.

With Charles still inside the hospital building, the coffin is at exactly 5.06 p.m., carried from the hospital by four pall-bearers. Covered in white lilies and gladioli, and watched by patients and a select number of press, it is carried out and placed in a blue Rivage hearse on which the blinds are drawn.

Charles leaves the hospital a few minutes later, and walks quickly towards his Jaguar. The convoy escorted by police moves off into the Paris traffic, the hearse being positioned sixth in the convoy. The way is opened up by police sirens, and two motorcycle film crews follow the cavalcade from the hospital to the airport. It's the Princess's last journey through Paris, and the most solemn of Charles' official visits to the foreign capital.

Charles' BAe 146 aircraft leaves direct for RAF Northolt, and Diana who had attempted suicide on five or six occasions is ironically returning in the same aircraft as the husband she was at such pains to divorce.

The aircraft on arrival is met by the Prime Minister, Tony Blair; who is part of a small party which numbers the Lord Chamberlain the Earl of Airlie, the Defence Secretary George Robertson and Lord Bramall, and the Lord Lieutenant of London. The coffin draped in the Royal Standard is shouldered across the tarmac by eight RAF pallbearers to the central building. With lightning efficiency the guarded coffin is left standing for a mere ten minutes before being conveyed to a hearse and driven away to a private mortuary.

With the same pre-planned efficiency Charles thanks those on hand, and boards his aircraft for the flight back to Aberdeen, and thence to join his sons at Balmoral. Charles' face expresses the opinion that a bad end for Diana was inevitable and just a matter of time. It's the children who need his love and protection.

A similar journey of grief to Paris had been undertaken by Mohammed Al Fayed, the Egyptian-born owner of the Harrods empire. His strongest dream for his first-born child was that he would marry Princess Diana, and so bring the considerable wealth of the Spencers into line with the Al Fayeds. Dodi's flamboyant lifestyle had matched Diana's in terms of their both being the black sheep of distinguished families. Both had rebelled against their upbringings, and had pursued the lifestyles of the mega-rich.

Mr. Al Fayed had received news of the disaster just before 1 a.m. on the Sunday morning at his Barrow Green Court estate in Surrey. He had immediately flown by private helicopter to Le Bourget airport, the place where Dodi and Diana had arrived twelve hours earlier with such romantic expectations.

Mr. Al Fayed is in the course of his distraught 75-minute flight determined to find scapegoats for the accident. Events like this are not allowed to happen to the privileged. On landing at Le Bourget airport he is driven to the hospital, and spends hours by his dead son's bedside. One accident witness has reported that Dodi's body had been twisted like a rag doll as a consequence of the head-on collision. He negotiates with the powers that be to have his son's body released and issues a statement through Harrods to the effect that: "This is an appalling and quite needless tragedy. The world has lost a Princess who is simply irreplaceable. Dodi was a kind, gentle and decent person who cheered the lives of those who knew him. He had a tremendous regard for Princess Diana and he cherished her friendship." Mr. Fayed's press officer added: "There is no doubt in Mr. Al Fayed's mind that this tragedy would not have occurred but for the press photographers who have dogged and pursued Mr. Fayed and the Princess for weeks. This sort of pursuit is entirely unacceptable. The Fayed family and the Princess's family put up with the press in St Tropez with good humour but they should not have had to endure such intrusion which cannot be justified."

As a mark of respect to the dead couple Mr. Al Fayed has the 11,000 light bulbs which illuminate Harrods switched off, but he will not consent to closing the store. Harrods is open for business as usual.

According to Muslim customs it is necessary that burial should take place within 24 hours of death. Dodi's body is promptly flown back to Britain on his father's private jet. The coffin is then taken to Regent's Park Mosque, where the large gathering of mourners participate in a simple service for the deceased. Dodi is then taken to Brookwood cemetery in Woking for a longer private family burial service. The couple's last 24 hours have implemented a state machinery that is seldom set in action.

Everything humanly possible has been done on both sides to ensure that the dead are treated with the utmost dignity and respect. Bureaucracy has been put into action with amazing speed, and to great effect. Diana awaits her burial, while Dodi has already been committed to a plot in Brookwood cemetery. Thunder has shaken Paris in the form of a heavy-duty Mercedes colliding at an estimated speed of 120 m.p.h. with a concrete pillar in the Alma underpass. Witnesses reported a bang that sounded like a terrorist attack. Many of them were so frightened by what they heard that they refused to come forward. Those who did offered conflicting reports. There was talk of a motorbike or a small car obstructing the Mercedes and causing the driver to swerve. Others claimed that the paparazzi were to blame, and that bikes weaving in and out of the car's path had caused the driver to loose control. Others attributed the crash to Henri Paul's alcohol. A victim had clearly to be found. In the Fayed circle there were accusations made that responsibilities for the accident lay with Muslim terrorists. Mr. Al Fayed suggested that the crash could have been the work of Muslim terrorists who were unwilling to condone Diana's relationship with Dodi. Diana's brother Earl Spencer held the press personally responsible for the Princess's death, despite there being no conclusive evidence that the paparazzi were to blame. His rancour seemed aimed at settling scores with a press which had lost no opportunity in exposing his bad behaviour as it had been disclosed in divorce proceedings. But Diana in all her years of courting press attention had never been mistreated by the paparazzi. Many of them were on familiar terms with her, and these men carried cameras and not guns.

What emerged in the 24 hours after Diana's death was the usual head-hunting injustice of the authorities looking for someone to blame. The moralistic spiel issued by Diana's brother, Mr. Al Fayed and Tony Blair all reeked of the supposedly unimpeachable looking with a degree of over self-righteousness on the paparazzi. There were two areas of blame, both of them likely to achieve populist appeal. That the chauffeur Henri Paul was three times over the drink-drive limit allowed the public to channel their anger on the driver. The paparazzi's part in the accident, something hugely overstated by the Fayeds and the

Spencers met with immediate public approval. Who better to blame than a drunk chauffeur and a pack of mercenary rats in pursuit of blood-money. They were easy targets. Tony Blair's opportunism had never known it so good. Attaching himself to a national spirit that verged on usurping the monarchy for the part they had played in demoting Diana, Blair's sham theatricals came into prominence. Unable ever to manifest sincerity, he was presented with an occasion on which insincerity would pass for genuine concern.

Blood tests conducted on Henri Paul showed he had drunk the equivalent of a bottle and a half of wine, and was three times over the French legal alcohol limit for driving. Tests on the body also revealed traces of the drug Prozac and smaller quantities of Triapide, a drug prescribed to combat alcoholic depression.

That Henri Paul had been expecting to remain off-duty on Saturday is something that should be taken into account. He was a regular drinker, a bon vivant who enjoyed his wine and whisky, and his intake that night was unlikely to affect his judgement at the wheel. The ride home to Dodi's flat was a short one, and Paul appeared sober to his colleagues at the Ritz. It was Dodi who decided that Paul should drive and that his regular chauffeur should trick the paparazzi by sitting in a parked decoy car. This wasn't after all such a monumental decision. The drive from the Ritz to the Champs Elysées should have occupied twenty minutes. It was a nothing job. Two people were going home, they wished to preserve their privacy, the press weren't there to murder them, and Dodi had Paul drive.

Paul's doctor in his home town of Lorient was unaware that his patient had a drink problem. Paul was not a dysfunctional alcoholic. While the drugs he had taken, Prozac and Triapide Hydrochloride can affect driving ability, Paul had undoubtedly developed a tolerance to his cocktail of alcohol and drugs. The war-cry that Diana was driven to her death by an irresponsible drunkard, a clamour taken up by the British tabloids, seemed too hasty and too short-sighted a conclusion to the day's events.

That Paul compartmentalized his life, separating his friends, seldom drinking for too long at any one bar, and keeping his private life to himself had made him something of an outsider. He was reported to be hard working and respected. He was a creature of routine, and whatever his drinking habits his exhaustive 60-page autopsy showed no liver deterioration of the kind associated with long-term alcoholism. In addition, he held a pilot's licence, and according to the woman with whom he had lived for five years, "his professional conscientiousness was irreproachable." This ex-lover also stressed of Paul, "his self-control was very impressive – he loved to be in charge of the situation and had great plans."

Paul was evidently neurotic, and as a cigar smoker he had on the Thursday before his death had his chest X-rayed at the Centre Radiologique Palais Royal, a private clinic in Paris. His worries were groundless, and he was given a clean bill of health. He was known also to have started a new relationship with a petite blonde woman, and to be optimistic about his future. Police discovered an empty bottle of white Martini in his flat, and an unopened bottle of champagne in the fridge. Paul was clearly a responsible Ritz employee who liked a drink in his leisure hours, but was hardly a legless drunk. From being a perfectly diligent and respectable citizen, Paul had within a space of hours subsequent to the crash become the most hated man in Europe. His corpse was unable to answer the vilification heaped on him by a blood-hungry nationalistic press. It's the belief of this writer that Paul was not to blame for what happened in the Alma Tunnel, but was forced to drive recklessly by his employer. It seems unlikely that Paul who was renowned for his self-control would drive into the Alma underpass at a speed of 110 m.p.h. without express orders to do so. Paul was not in a position to disobey his employer, or take risks for which he alone was accountable. Members of the Fayed staff obey orders, and do not dictate at what speed a car is driven. It would not have been worth Paul's job if he had driven away from the Ritz at a speed with which Dodi was uncomfortable. There was plenty of time after Paul jumped a red light -- and before it too -- for Dodi to have told his driver to cool it. We remember Diana's terror earlier in the day when she had been driven in from Le Bourget airport at speeds which appeared highly dangerous. She had asked the driver to slow down, but Dodi had overridden her request. Nobody would drive a member of the Fayed family at suicidal speed into an underpass, without their consent or encouragement. Was Dodi intent on killing everyone in the car, including himself? Did he perhaps realise that Diana wasn't right for him, or he for her, and so decided to perversely kill the whole thing in a spectacular way?

The press aren't so terrifying a proposition that a car has to risk crashing in the get away. The estimated fifteen motorcyclists in pursuit of the Mercedes were hundreds of yards behind the car, and only Romauld Rat was driving a bike fast enough to overtake the limousine. He was the first to arrive at the crash, but even he was an estimated 300 yards behind the speeding car.

Paul had that week purchased a new camera, and before the fatal journey, he had wandered out of the front entrance of the Ritz and asked Rat's advice about which flash to buy. Paul was on good terms with the paparazzi, and so partly was Diana, and the idea of a car crashing into a pillar simply to elude the press appears ridiculous. What did the couple have to hide that this journey should have taken on such monumental proportions? It was well-known that they were dating, but it's not as if they were having open sex in the rear of the car. Why was there such an urgency to get back to Dodi's apartment? They were after all staying in the £6,000 a night Imperial Suite at the Ritz, and surely could have made themselves adequately comfortable for what was to be a single night. Why at 12.20 a.m. did Dodi consider it so important that they left the hotel to which they had retired to find the privacy denied them elsewhere?

In the immediate attempt to blame Paul and/or the paparazzi for the accident, none of these questions were raised. One of Paul's old friends was reported as saying: "He was an accomplished professional driver. No-one can believe what has been written about him." Still another said: "I have known him for 15 years. He had a good job. He liked his job and he liked life. Now I've got a friend who is dead." These quiet undemonstrative statements were in sharp contrast to the unanimous press verdict that Paul had virtually murdered Diana. Another close colleague gave the opinion that: "The image of him as an irresponsible drunk is totally false. He drank, but not to excess. I don't think he had a drink problem. To have done what he did in life, it is obvious that he was a serious person. You could tell from the way he talked that he was a serious person." Nothing was made of the fact that Paul had been a captain when he left the military in 1984, and that he regularly hired a private aircraft to fly from Paris to his parent's house in Lorient at the weekends. To hold a pilot's licence Paul underwent regular check-ups, and there was never any question of his being unfit to fly. A lot of drivers on the road that night would have consumed as much or more alcohol than Paul, but returned safely home. It wasn't Paul's judgements that were in error, the fault may have been with the probable instructions he was receiving. Nobody questioned how much Dodi and Diana had drunk that night, or their use of recreational drugs in the course of their evening at the

Ritz. The possible irresponsibility of the car's passengers seemed never to have been considered. It was much easier to blame the driver and a bunch of mercenary paparazzi. Diana and Dodi would be vindicated at their expense.

That Paul was drunk needs no additional confirmation. Ian Hindmarch, of Surrey University, an authority on the effects of alcohol and drugs on driving ability gave his opinion that "if the driver had not had a drink the drugs would have had little effect. We are not talking about someone who was pretty thoroughly intoxicated." Hindmarch also added that "at a level of 180 mg the crash risk is between 15 and 150 times more than it would be for a non-drinker."

Little too was made of the fact that Rees-Jones had fastened his seatbelt just prior to the car's entering the tunnel. It is rare that bodyguards wear seatbelts for it hinders their abilities to protect their clients. Was Rees-Jones shocked into this action by Dodi's commands that Paul should increase speed, or did he know what was coming? The conspiracy theory that the Princess was murdered by British agents out of anti-Arab racist feelings, was a theory raised by millions of Arabs, including Dodi's father.

One of the leading columnists for the Egyptian daily Al Ahram, expressed the belief that Diana was the victim of a British-inspired conspiracy. Without mincing his words he wrote: "she was killed by British Intelligence to save the monarchy... Nobody since Cromwell, who called for a republic in the 17th century, has been able to shake the Royal Family as Princess Diana did."

Another columnist wrote: "I and many of my friends are convinced that the brakes of the car were tampered with by British agents paid by the Queen. She did not want the possibility of half-Arab children getting close to the Crown."

The viewpoint that Diana's death was engineered was given additional fuel by Colonel Gaddafi's anti-western regime in Tripoli. Libyan radio broadcast the belief that "only children believe that it was an accident." The Arabs found further cause for their conspiracy theory by claiming that the British Establishment had been at great pains to prevent Dodi's father, Mohammed Al Fayed, from securing British citizenship.

Was Diana as an individual really so powerful that she merited assassination? That she possessed a faculty for self-promotion rarely seen in a woman since Jacqueline Kennedy Onassis, helped mask the issue that her real talents in the political world were slight, if any. If her marriage to Charles had proved a happy one, it's doubtful she would have been remembered at all. The anti-landmines campaign that she had fostered in the last months of her life seemed like an attempt on her part to gain public sympathy at the expense of the Royals. It's unlikely that Diana was ever truly regarded as the People's Princess during her lifetime. She was as much disliked for her self-publicity campaigns, as she was admired for her work with charities. It was Tony Blair who sensing the movement was right, seized on this caption, and used it both to his own and the nation's advantage.

Conspiracy theories continue to abound, and whether Rees-Jones will in time remember anything of value to add light to the events, remains to be seen. The responsibility for Diana's death would also seem to rest in part with whoever advised her to trust the Fayeds and not her own security system. But perhaps we can ascribe her deficient security to romance. It was after all Diana's summer of passionate love. She was dizzy with what had begun as a fling and deepened into an acceptance on her part to marry Dodi Fayed. She was an insecure woman looking for love and she seemed at last to have found it. It wasn't everyone's idea of the perfect match, and it may have been another act of rebellion on Diana's part, but for a short time it had seemed to do the trick. Diana was smiling and Dodi looked like a cat who had licked the cream. And what of the possible outcome of this union? Dodi's rather pointless existence as a playboy would presumably have found acceptance by his father, and Diana would have added further insult to the Queen by marrying a playboy. Both parties would have benefited by a sensational and probably equally short-lived marriage. The general public would quickly have grown bored with yet another item of news in Diana's portfolio, and the British would have resented her marrying a Muslim. Diana thrived on controversy, and her highly privileged position allowed her to do as she liked. Part of the responsibility for the crash should be placed on her shoulders. She knew precisely the risk she was taking in renouncing her private security, and in placing her life in the hands of a man who was addicted to fast cars and an equally fast lifestyle. After her stagnant marriage to Charles it was understandable that she should seek pleasure with a man who was in every respect his opposite. It was the petulant, anti-establishment side of Diana had her take up with Dodi. It was her chance to show the Royal Family that she could hold her own with a mega-rich hedonist known for his irresponsible lifestyle. Diana needed a new publicity theme, and Dodi served the bill. This was her chance to put her fingers up at the Balmoral lot, and prove her independence. Diana for all her presumed worldliness was like most of her class naive, and in thinking that she could take on a man versed in pleasure, she fell prey to her vulnerabilities. Why else we ask would she have been seated in the rear of a Mercedes driven at 120 m.p.h. across Paris without cause to justify that speed? It was her naivety that put her in such a life-threatening situation, and ultimately proved her undoing.

Dodi's father Mohammed Al-Fayed was a close friend of the late Lord Spencer, the Princess's father. In some respects Diana shared more in common with Mohammed Al-Fayed than she did with Dodi. They both felt like outsiders. Diana believed that she was disliked by the Royal Family, and Fayed had been branded a liar in a Department of Trade and Industry report into his takeover of Harrods. Fayed despite his being championed by Margaret Thatcher was none-theless shunned by the British establishment. But Diana who spent much of her shopping time in Harrods had a soft spot for Fayed, and would have an audience with the owner whenever she visited the store. If Dodi had married Diana, Mohammed would have found admission to the royal circle, and been granted British citizenship. It was little wonder that Mohammed had played matchmaker in bringing the couple together. They had both been divorced, and were young enough to begin new lives and have a family. He had invited the two to share a Mediterranean holiday with him on board his schooner Sikara. According to Diana it was the best holiday she had ever known. "We are all sitting here having withdrawal symptoms," she had told a friend on the telephone.

There is every reason to believe that Diana was temporarily taken over by the

Fayeds. Her father Earl Spencer had asked Mohammed to keep an eye on the family, and the carrying out of that request was indirectly why she found herself in the back seat of a Mercedes being driven madly across Paris in the early hours of September 1st 1997. It's also hard to know how much real importance Diana attached to her relationship with Dodi. Throughout her life Diana had won attention for making her insecurities public. Were the Fayeds simply offering the Princess the security that she claimed her marriage had been without? Would Diana have disengaged herself from the affair at a later date, despite her acceptance of Dodi's proposal. These are uncertain speculations, for Diana and Dodi were both unstable in relationships, and both possessed the wealth necessary to pamper their fantasies. It's just as likely that Diana after having got her own back on the Royals would have regretted her decision to marry.

It wasn't as if Dodi was a remarkable catch. Yes, he would have succeeded his father as emperor of Harrods, but he had a reputation for gambling, bouncing cheques, and was sued repeatedly for his failure to pay rent on several luxury homes in Southern California. He generally left his father to clean up the mess. Dodi collected celebrities and beautiful women, and his marriage to Suzanne Gregard in 1986 was quickly followed by a divorce settlement costing more than £2m. Diana, whose taste in men was always deplorable, seems to have been attracted to the cad in Dodi. Dodi was well known for his habit of dispatching his girlfriends back home with a one-way ticket on what they jokingly referred to as Air Dodi. Dodi was a minor figure in international gossip, who like Diana was over-rich, and had never devoted himself to a single cause. In fact during the time that Dodi was having his summer fling with Diana, an American model, Kelly Fisher, proclaimed that she was engaged to Dodi, and had a ring, and a mutually-agreed wedding date – 9 August. Fisher also claimed to have been given a pay-off from Dodi in the form of a cheque for $200,000, which had subsequently bounced. Dodi's flippancy with regard to relationships would have boded ill for Diana whose own short-lived affairs had brought her little happiness.

Dodi's bad track record and his unsuitability as a potential husband to Diana would fuel the idea of a British conspiracy theory. But was Diana really so important to the British public? Her canonization largely occurred after her death. Tabloids like the News of the World, who had run an acid feature on the relationship of Diana to her sons, published on the day she died, quickly presented a turn-about front to their readers. The nation rose proclaiming Diana a saint, irrespective of the fact that she had done little to earn a sainthood. The care she had expressed over Aids sufferers had always reeked of opportunism. Her charities had formed the main front of her publicity drive, but she had intended to abandon the lot after meeting Dodi, and to retire from public life. There was something in Diana of the retarded teenager ever ready to shock if she couldn't get her own way. Not powerful enough in her lifetime to bring about an end to the monarchy, she and Fergie provoked scandals the like of which the Royal Family had never known. Both women for good or bad made public areas of their personal lives which the Queen thought shocking. The archaic institution of monarchy, obsolete itself in the twentieth century had survived by maintaining its seemingly flawless protocol. The Queen and Prince Philip had been the subject of no major scandal, whereas Diana and Ferguson seemed intent on airing their dirty washing in public. In Charles' words, they had succeeded in making the Royal Family into the biggest soap opera on earth. In her death Diana came close to bringing about the downfall of the monarchy. The anti-royalist feelings inspired by her death, and by the repressed anger of a mob who blamed the Queen for having demoted Diana, was successful in bringing about almost immediate and necessary reforms to the monarchy. Diana's death was indirectly blamed on the monarchy. The feeling shared by the crowd was that Diana had been driven to a state of neurotic recklessness because she had suffered mistreatment at the hands of the Royals. But how would that same media-informed crowd have responded had Diana lived to marry an unsuitable playboy? The Guardian wasted no words in dismissing Dodi's contribution to life by claiming "His last days were dogged by the further tackiness of dodging the media."

On the night of August 31, 1997, three occupants travelling in a Mercedes limousine were killed when the car slammed into a concrete pillar in the Alma underpass.

People die every day in cars, but Diana's death was not allowed to be considered another road casualty. Other theories contributing to the crash were advanced largely because the public mourning Diana were unwilling to let her go. The newly exalted People's Princess had established herself in death as a contemporary icon. But what of the other theories. Unlike the Imperial Suite at the Ritz, Diana's car wasn't bugged. One theory made popular by Mohammed Al Fayed was that another car had swerved in front of Henri Paul, and so contributed to the crash. Eye witnesses claimed that a white Fiat Uno had swerved in front of the Mercedes and driven it off the road. Al Fayed's own investigating team, which included John MacNamara, formerly of Scotland Yard, announced they had found the car which had been sold in November to a garage near Paris. It was claimed that the white Fiat Uno had been damaged on the left rear fender and had been repaired. Pierre Ottavioli, a French private eye in the Fayeds' employ claimed that the car had "belonged to a photo-journalist who was very interested in the Princess of Wales." There was apparently a streak of white paint found on the crashed Mercedes limousine, evidence disclaimed by the French police.

According to the eyewitness report of François Levy, a former harbour pilot, who entered the tunnel ahead of Diana and Dodi's car, he claims to have seen in his rear-view mirror, a motorbike swerve in front of the car just before the crash. According to Levy's account he saw the headlights of the Mercedes zigzag as he was leaving the tunnel. He heard a huge bang like a bomb explosion, and pulled over to the side of the road. Levy says he wanted to go back to the scene, but his wife was frightened, and pleaded with him to drive off. Levy failed to mention a slow-moving white Fiat Uno being ahead of the Mercedes, which swerved to avoid it. Police investigators do not regard Levy's account as wholly reliable. Witnesses who arrived at the scene of the crash vary in their reports as to the number of photographers taking shots of the crash. One witness claimed there were no more than two or three photographers on site, while two police officers who arrived on scene at 12.30 stated, "the camera flashes were going off like machinegun fire around the back right-hand side of the vehicle where the door was open." One reporter is alleged to have shouted to the officer: "You're pissing me off. Let me do my work." Another joined in and said: "Yeah, go to Bosnia, then you'll see how we do our work." But according to Frederic Mailliez who was tending to the dying Diana, the photographers at no time attempted to impede his work. Mailliez stated: "I was aware that people were taking photographs while I worked. I could feel flashes going on around me. But they didn't get in my way." According to Mailliez Diana was groaning and mumbling, but he could not make out what she was saying.

If according to Mohammed Al Fayed there was a conspiracy to murder, then the paparazzi were surely without motivation. The press need their celebrities alive and not dead. If there is a legitimate conspiracy theory in the events of that night, it is that the establishment did not want the mother of the future King marrying a Muslim of no real social status. If there was a plot, then the situation favoured it. Diana was without her own security guards and the Alma Tunnel, with its tricky entrance was an ideal spot for a serious accident. But there was no assurance that Diana wouldn't be wearing her seatbelt. Experts have claimed that she would have survived the crash if she had fastened her seatbelt. Are we to assume that Diana was told it was unnecessary to take this precaution, or equally possible was Diana on a substance that rendered her behaviour irresponsible? Had Dodi encouraged the Princess to take cocaine with him in their private suite at the Ritz? The author would suggest that the latter theory is a distinct possibility amongst the many theories advanced as to the sequence of events that night. Irresponsibility on Diana and Dodi's parts may well have been the prime cause of the fatal crash. Far more so than the idea rumoured by the Fayeds that Diana's death was a textbook example of how secret services force accidents to happen.

In the authorized witchhunt succeeding the crash, six photographers and a motorcycle courier were faced with manslaughter charges. The men were Jacques Langevin, 45, Romauld Rat, 30, Christian Martinez, 35, and who took the photos of John Bryan toe-sucking the Duchess of York, Nicholas Arsov, 30, Serge Arnal, 35, Laszlo Verez, 48, and the Ganna driver Stéphane Darmon, 30. All seven were released on bail the following night, September 2, 1997, but were suspended from work. Georges Kiejman by way of prosecution put forward the Fayeds' case that "there was a chase without which the driver would never have taken that route nor used that speed." The defence claimed that "if the victims had not been of such exceptional quality this litigation would never have been brought with such theatricality. I hope that the situation will become more calm."

We know from the report given by Stéphane Darmon, one of the accused, that prior to the chase to the tunnel, events as the photographers waited for the couple outside the Ritz bordered on good humour. Darmon stated: "Henri Paul began playing games with us, saying that they would be out in 10 minutes, then five. He staged two false departures, in which Mercedes cars drove round Place Vendôme and came back again. He laughed at us charging off behind them, and the crowd enjoyed it too. In retrospect, he was overly jolly but I did not think about it at the time, especially since I had no idea he would end up driving Diana and Dodi's car."

Darmon also denied that Henri Paul issued a challenge to the paparazzi, and claims that all the car's windows were closed on the short journey to the underpass. He remembers seeing Diana in the rear of the car still wearing dark sunglasses. He stated too that the bikers were at a considerable disadvantage to the Mercedes' speed, and that they were left so far behind the car that they had almost abandoned the chase.

Subsequent investigations into the crash have suggested that Henri Paul may have been working for the French secret service for years and was paid an unexplained £4,000 a month. Paul enjoyed a lifestyle beyond that which his salary at the Ritz would have permitted, and his job brought him into contact with celebrities and politicians. Even more mysterious is the claim made by an ITV documentary that blood samples taken from Henri Paul contained more that 20 per cent of carbon monoxide – as well as alcohol. Doctors concluded that Paul must have been exposed to the gas before getting into the Mercedes, and that his mental judgement would have been severely impaired. No traces of carbon monoxide were found in Dodi Fayed's blood. Are we to presume that Paul was exposed to the gas by a member of British intelligence, or by a journalist? Or are we to conclude that he inhaled the gas in order to get himself high? Still another theory holds that Paul was temporarily blinded by a laser pen shone into his eyes by a motorcyclist. Paul's friends, one of them a barman at the Ritz claimed he was stone cold sober that night, and there is a tenable theory that blood samples were switched by M16 in the Paris mortuary with the intention of showing that Paul was drunk.

If British intelligence had wished to murder Dodi Fayed, then they risked killing Diana in the same operation. James Hewitt, whose much publicised affair with Diana had raged across the tabloid headlines was visited by M15 and told that if he didn't stop seeing her he would meet the same fate as Barry Mannakee – a police bodyguard who became close to the Princess and died in an unexplained motorcycle accident in 1986.

Further mystery clues have arisen in connection with the route taken by Henri Paul that night. It was not the normal way used by drivers, and there was no necessity for him to use the Alma tunnel in the drive to Dodi's apartment. According to staff at the Ritz they were called together two days after the crash and told to cover up the truth by not admitting that Henri Paul was drunk. Mohammed Al Fayed had masterminded his son's relationship with Diana, and had apparently ordered him to give precedence to Diana and to drop Kelly Fisher to whom he was to be married in August 1997. That

Mohammed as owner of the Ritz failed to provide adequate security for Diana on the night she died, would account for his propaganda campaign to deflect any responsibility for Diana's death. Apart from bugging suites at the Ritz, Al Fayed's residences in Mayfair and St. Tropez were also reportedly bugged, and Diana's intimate life was recorded in all three places.

There are facts and abundant conspiracy theories, but none of them quite add up. It is claimed that vital video evidence has never been passed on to the authorities, and that Ritz footage of Paul and fellow driver Frederic Lucas has been destroyed. Presumably video evidence would have shown that Henri Paul was drunk before he got into the car.

The French authorities claim still to

have discovered no major findings. If Diana hadn't been a celebrity would these endless conspiracy theories exist? Probably not. Very few cars crashes excite this sort of attention, and no-one is prepared to take the blame for the accident. Michael Cole, Fayed's chief spokesman, alleged that the crash was caused by photographers firing flashguns through the car's windscreen after it had left the Ritz. According to Michael Cole, and there is no evidence to substantiate his claim: "Henri Paul was dazzled by a flash, while Trevor Rees-Jones was lowering the sun-visor to protect himself from the photographers and Princess Diana was hiding her face in her arms." According to Cole the Mercedes was "like a Wells Fargo Stagecoach surrounded by Indians."

But in reality is anyone really that

scared of being photographed? Diana had spent her life in front of flashguns and had welcomed the attention. It was the paparazzi who were responsible for making her the most photographed member of the Royal Family. Why should Diana have been hiding her face in her arms?

Another theory advanced by Fayed's detractors is that Trevor Rees-Jones as the only survivor of the crash, also caused the accident. Could Rees-Jones, who was sitting next to Henri Paul have administered the carbon monoxide found in Paul's blood? According to Debbie Davis, of the Leeds-based Carbon Monoxide Support Group, the gas deprives the brain of oxygen, and "you can't judge distance and you can't judge time." If Henri Paul had been exposed to the gas just prior to entering the tunnel, then he would have undoubtedly have lost control of the powerful car. It would have accounted for the car's swerving before crashing into a pillar. Rees-Jones it should be remembered was not employed by Diana, but was part of the Fayed protection team. If the blood samples proving more than 20 per cent of carbon monoxide were indeed from Paul, then it's assumed he would have been incapable of walking, let alone driving a car. The obvious conclusion then is that he was given carbon monoxide in the course of the journey. The question, like everything else surrounding the crash remains open.

In late August 1998, renegade MI6 agent Richard Tomlinson gave a 2-hour interview behind the closed doors of the Palais de Justice, allegedly detailing "possible MI6 involvement" in Diana's death. No details have emerged at time of writing.

Bugging devices at Dodi's apartment and at the Imperial Suite go to show that although the couple appeared to have found a brief summer happiness, all was not well. Diana was hugely jealous of the other women in Dodi's life, and knew him to be unfaithful. Tantrums thrown by Diana in her final hours suggest a desperately insecure woman clinging to an unsuitable lover, rather than risk losing him. At one time Diana can be heard saying, "I don't care about those other bitches, you'll find I'm better in bed than all of them." Diana's attraction to Dodi seems to have been sexual. It was her summer of rebellion, and Dodi Fayed fitted the bill by way of her raising two fingers at the establishment.

Throughout her life Diana had been attracted not to real value, but to the super-rich, and to those who have been called representatives of a fake society. Diana associated largely with media personalities: Versace, and Will Carling. Diana seemed never to penetrate beyond the superficial to a deeper understanding of life. That Diana should be commemorated in death by Elton John's cloyingly sentimental "Candle In The Wind" seemed the final ironic comment on her values.

What happened in the last four minutes of Diana's life will always be open to speculation. The key to the accident lies with the speed at which the car was driven. Conflicting reports have claimed that the car slowed down to 100 m.p.h. 80 yards before entering the tunnel, but the vehicle was still travelling fast. The slightest order from his employer would have corrected the speed at which Henri Paul was driving. Four minutes is a long time in which to be made uncomfortable by a chauffeur. Even if Diana did protest at the speed and Dodi overruled her, there was still time for Dodi to think again. Henri Paul was a regular drinker, and the idea of him taking off on an unauthorized drink-and-drive rampage is ludicrous. The paparazzi reported on how skilfully Paul had weaved his way through traffic to the red light. He was driving well and was undoubtedly in full control of the car. Paul's judgement wasn't the problem. He did what he was told to do, and that is to pile on the speed. If Dodi had told him to drive slow he would have driven slow.

None of the three men in the car

were answerable to Diana. Nobody seemed to have questioned if one of the three men intended to die and take the others with him. Diana wanted to live, as far as we know Rees-Jones didn't have a death-wish, nor Henri Paul, despite his treatment for depression. Dodi Fayed's death-wish was an unconscious one, and it came out in his love of speed. When the car smashed into the concrete pillar, he had dared it to its fatal limits.